APPLIQUÉ MASTERPIECE
Series

Birds 'n' ROSES

Margaret Docherty

American Quilter's Society
P. O. Box 3290 • Paducah, KY 42002-3290
www.AmericanQuilter.com

PHOTO: KEITH LEEMING

Located in Paducah, Kentucky, the American Quilter's Society (AQS) is dedicated to promoting the accomplishments of today's quilters. Through its publications and events, AQS strives to honor today's quiltmakers and their work and to inspire future creativity and innovation in quiltmaking.

EDITOR: BARBARA SMITH
GRAPHIC DESIGN: ELAINE WILSON
COVER DESIGN: MICHAEL BUCKINGHAM
PHOTOGRAPHY: CHARLES R. LYNCH, UNLESS NOTED OTHERWISE

PHOTO: KEITH LEEMING

Library of Congress Cataloging-in-Publication Data
Docherty, Margaret.
    Appliqué masterpiece series. Birds 'n roses / by Margaret Docherty.
    p. cm.
  Summary: "Complete pattern for prize-winning quilt, Birds 'n Roses. Projects include a section on building a garden quilt design, a description of the real flowers and birds portrayed in quilt, suggestions for fabric selection, and instructions for embellishment. Also contains ideas for simplifying the original quilt design--Provided by publisher."
    ISBN 1-57432-914-6 (alk. paper)
    1. Appliqué--Patterns. 2. Quilting--Patterns. 3. Quilts. I. Title.

TT779.D633 2006
746.46'041--dc22

                                    2006032752

Additional copies of this book may be ordered from the American Quilter's Society, PO Box 3290, Paducah, KY 42002-3290; 800-626-5420 (orders only please); or online at www.AmericanQuilter.com. For all other inquiries, call 270-898-7903.

Dedication

To Margaret Martin Glover, my late mother, with a lifetime of fond memories

PHOTO: KEITH LEEMING

Acknowledgments

My thanks …

to the makers of the modern Garden Quilts:

Zena Thorpe   FROGMORE

Karen Kay Buckley   MEMORIES OF THE HOLIDAYS

Shoko Ferguson   MY BLUE GARDEN

Betty Ekern Suiter   WELCOME TO MY DREAMS

Keiko Miyauchi   BLUE EARTH WITH WATER AND FLOWERS

for their help and support:

Roderick Kiracofe

The Quilter's Hall of Fame

for their photos:

Sue Tranter, suesbirdphotos.co.uk

Keith Leeming, National Auricula and Primula Society, UK

Peter Grencis, Head of Medical Photography & Illustration
University Hospital of North Durham, UK

Contents

BIRDS 'N' ROSES, 84" x 84", by the author. This quilt won two best of show awards in 2005, at the American Quilter's Society and National Quilting Association shows.

Margaret Docherty

Preface

BIRDS 'N' ROSES started life sometime in the late summer of 1999. It was initially intended to be a floral medallion quilt with a central cream circular panel, appliquéd into a royal blue background and decorated with filigree gold appliqué. I wanted it to resemble a decorative floral bone china plate, with a heavily ornate floral center surrounded by rich royal blue and decorated with gold.

Many quilters will say that a quilt has a mind of its own and determines its own design. BIRDS 'N' ROSES was given a lot of help in escaping the original plan—my idée fixe about auriculas, lots of auriculas. The auricula and polyanthus border was designed before any other part of the quilt. From there on, the auriculas determined the rest of the quilt.

I deferred designing the outer appliqué and started sewing the auricula border. By autumn it was well under way when I traveled to the International Quilting Association show, "Quilts: A World of Beauty," in Houston, Texas. This was a memorable occasion for me because my quilt LITTLE BROWN BIRD had won best in show. It was equally memorable for an amazing exhibition of the 100 best American quilts of the twentieth century. I had difficulty in tearing myself away from them.

On the long flight home, I was browsing the pages of the book published in conjunction with the exhibition. In the early hours of the morning, some 25,000 feet above the North Atlantic, I realized I was making a Garden Quilt.

Garden Quilts reached a peak of popularity in the second quarter of the last century. There are no less than four of them in the selection of the 100 best. They were acknowledged to be show stoppers when displayed at quilt shows, and to complete a winning Garden Quilt was described as the acme of the maker's quilting career.

I planned to call my version NEW MILLENNIUM GARDEN, but time passed all too quickly; the new millennium overtook me! I had started sewing BIRDS 'N' ROSES in 1999 but finished it nearly five years later.

Any brave persons wanting to replicate BIRDS 'N' ROSES should be aware that they are in for a long haul. This is not a "quick quilt."

Birds 'n' Roses was designated a masterpiece quilt at the National Quilting Association annual show in 1995, when Margaret became the seventeenth member of the Master Quilter's Guild.

Introduction

American Quilter's Society published my first book, *Masterpiece Appliqué, Little Brown Bird Patterns,* in 2000. Since then, many Little Brown Bird Quilts have been made. I have listened to the stories of many quilters who have reproduced this Baltimore-style Album quilt and have been delighted to see quilters winning awards with their own LITTLE BROWN BIRDS around the world. Five years later, I am told that quilters are now ready for a Garden Quilt, an even longer quilting odyssey.

BIRDS 'N' ROSES is a time-taking project. I would hope beginners are not tempted to become involved with making a replica of this quilt, but will rather dip into the individual flower and bird patterns and use them on less time-consuming projects. A novice needs to have the satisfaction and reward of finishing several projects fairly quickly. Several of the flower and leaf designs are quite easy appliqué pieces to start with, the clematis being a good example. I hope that novice quilters will enjoy the book for its pictures and patterns and perhaps as an inspiration for the future.

I believe an intermediate or advanced quilter is more likely to get to grips with making a Garden Quilt. With this in mind, I have omitted very basic appliqué and quiltmaking instructions, which I did include in the LITTLE BROWN BIRD book.

There is a section on how to build up a Garden Quilt design. Pictures of old and new Garden Quilts are included to give the reader further inspiration. I would love to see a Garden Quilt revival in the not too distant future with many new quilts showing dazzling arrays of flowers and swags.

I have also included a section describing the real flowers and birds portrayed in the quilt, comparing them with the fabric reproductions and giving examples and suggestions for the fabric selection.

The patterns themselves are large scale, and several pattern pieces must be joined together to make a complete pattern. Instructions are included on how to join the pattern pieces together. Simpler alternative patterns are also provided, which eliminate the more time-consuming elements of the original quilt design.

Even if you don't plan to make a Garden Quilt, I hope you will enjoy the illustrations and descriptive text and find the technical information a useful source of reference.

CHAPTER 1

A Garden Quilt

Margaret Docherty

A Potted History of the Garden Quilt

BIRDS 'N' ROSES is not dissimilar to a genre of quilts made in the 1930s known as Garden Quilts. It will take a very long time to construct, and perhaps the process might be made easier by the knowledge that others have been there before you.

Arsinoe Kelsey Bowen, a minister's wife living in Cortland, New York, finished a quilt in 1857. A skilled needlewoman, with more than a flair for design, her quilt was exceptional. It is likely that this quilt was much admired by local ladies and was renowned in the quilting community, long before the days of quilting books or quilt shows and competitions. It is not known what name Mrs. Bowen gave to her quilt if, indeed, it had a name.

Over half a century later, the first book about quilts was published. In 1915, Marie Daugherty Webster published her famous book *Quilts: Their Story and How to Make Them.* Mrs. Webster showed pictures of many historic quilts and many new ones, designed by herself, to a new generation of quilters. She wrote about techniques, discussed design, and marketed the patterns for her designs. This was a landmark for quilters, and it promoted a surge of interest in quiltmaking.

Although many beautiful appliquéd quilts appeared in Mrs. Webster's book, there were none quite the same as that made by Arsinoe Kelsey Bowen. It was more than a decade later that a picture of Mrs. Bowen's quilt was available to quilters. A four-inch-square black and white photograph of the quilt appeared as an illustration in the 1929 book *Old Patchwork Quilts and the Women Who Made Them,* by Ruth Finley.

Ruth Finley (1884–1955), an early feminist, originally worked in the newspaper business. She developed an interest in quilters and promoted quilting as a women's folk art. She traveled the country collecting stories and quilt patterns from quilters. It was Mrs. Finley who discovered the Bowen quilt. At the time, a great niece of Mrs. Bowen owned the quilt. Its whereabouts today is unknown.

It may be that Ruth Finley was responsible for naming the Bowen quilt a Garden Quilt. Finley's contacts with the newspaper industry ensured good publicity for her book, which was very popular.

There is no pattern for the Bowen quilt in Mrs. Finley's book, but the text accompanying the small picture extols the virtues of the quilt most eloquently and at great length. Mrs. Finley concluded her praise by claiming that none but a very few of even the most talented quilters could produce such a masterpiece.

This comment must have been as a red cape to a bull to experienced quilters. I would think that this comment alone was responsible for many Garden Quilts being made in the 1930s. Ruth Finley had thrown down the gauntlet, and many met the challenge.

RED BIRDS (1938), 86" x 97", by Katurah Elizabeth Tooley. Photo courtesy of Roderick Kiracofe, from *The American Quilt: A History of Cloth and Comfort 1750–1950* (Clarkson N. Potter, 1993). PHOTO: SHARON RISEDORPH.

Margaret Docherty

The great Garden Quilt revival occurred in the 1930s and 1940s with quilters fiercely competing at quilt shows to produce the best Garden Quilt. Those wanting to produce their own versions of this quilt had to devise ways of copying from a small picture.

Katurah Elizabeth Tooley, who made a Garden Quilt named as one of the best 100 American quilts of the twentieth century, received help from her husband who projected the image for her, allowing her to trace a pattern from the projection. Mrs. Tooley named her quilt RED BIRDS, page 11.

Mrs. Tooley's quilt is similar to the original Bowen quilt, but she added her own individual touch by replacing the blue birds in the border with red cardinals, hence the name RED BIRDS.

Arsinoe Bowen's quilt is 96 inches square. Mrs. Tooley's version is 86 by 97 inches. The original quilt has virtually no plain border beyond the outer appliqué. Mrs. Tooley left an area of plain fabric on all sides beyond the appliqué but added more at the top and bottom of the quilt to create a rectangular finish. Presumably she intended it as a bed quilt. I know of no family members or friends whom I would allow to sleep under this masterpiece.

Woman's Day magazine eventually published a Garden Quilt pattern in 1943. The designer of the published pattern was Pine Hawkes Eisfeller. One of her Garden Quilts is also among the 100 best.

The ladies who quilted in Emporia, Kansas, in the 1930s were the most famous of the Garden Quilt brigade. A fiercely competitive group, they strove to surpass each other's attempts at making a Garden masterpiece. Two of these ladies were also honored in the final lineup of the best 100 quilts.

Josephine Emma Craig made a glorious Garden Quilt (1933), page 13, which received national acclaim. A detail of this quilt appears as a cover picture on the 1992 reprint of *Old-Fashioned Quilts and the Women Who Made Them.*

Mrs. Craig has used the general format of central medallion, swag, circular border with the original blue birds, and outer appliqué border. She added her own personal touch of bold flowers depicted in equally bold colors.

The person most remembered for her Garden Quilt is Rose Kretsinger (1886–1963). Much has been written about this most celebrated of Emporia, Kansas, quilters. She did not start quilting until she was 40 years old, but she had an art background, having studied at the Art Institute of Chicago.

She earned national renown when she co-authored the book *The Romance of the Patchwork Quilt in America* (Dover, 1989) with Carrie Hall in 1935. She was noted as a good and generous teacher as well as an accomplished quilter. A long series of winning quilts culminated in her ultimate triumph, PARADISE GARDEN, in 1946, page 14. This quilt was one of the seven juried into the best 100 American quilts on the first ballot by all the jurors.

GARDEN QUILT (ca. 1933), 86" x 85", by Josephine Emma Craig. From the collection of The Kansas State Historical Society. Photograph courtesy of the society.

Margaret Docherty

PARADISE GARDEN (1946), 93" x 94", by Rose Kretsinger, from the collection of the Spencer Museum of Art, The University of Kansas. Photo courtesy of the museum.

Margaret Docherty

The person who did the appliqué did not always complete the quilting on these masterpieces. Rose Kretsinger has a large feathered quilting motif named after her. Although she designed and freely gave her quilting patterns to others, she did not quilt her PARADISE GARDEN quilt. The quilter is unknown. The quilter of RED BIRDS is also not known.

Josephine Craig is said to have received help with both the design and the quilting on her Garden Quilt. Friends, Elizabeth Goering and Maud Leatherberry, helped her. The quilting was rated as 100 percent perfect by the judges at the 1933 Kansas State Fair.

Feathered quilting motif

What Is a Garden Quilt?

The Garden Quilts from the first half of the twentieth century all have the same format, which is based on the original quilt by Arsinoe Bowen.

The elements of a traditional Garden Quilt can be broken down as follows:

Central medallion. The medallion is symmetrical in form with four large flowers at the center. The four flowers spread out symmetrically in multiples of four.

Swag. The central medallion is contained by a swag. Arsinoe Bowen's swag has a clever three-dimensional appearance. Rose Kretsinger made a very elaborate swag trimmed with roses, which sets the center medallion off to perfection and leads the eye outward to the outer border. (See pages 113–115 for a pattern of a similar swag.)

Middle border. This is a circular area with less appliqué than the rest of the quilt. It is the ideal place to show off fancy quilting with trapunto.

Corner unit. The corner units serve to square the quilt, while continuing to mirror the circular shape.

Outer border. Quilts usually have plain outer borders of varying widths. A Garden Quilt is, in fact, just an appliquéd floral medallion with a particular border arrangement.

corner unit

central medallion

plain outer edge

circular border

swag

Typical Garden Quilt

MEMORIES OF THE HOLIDAYS, 92" x 92", by Karen Kay Buckley. Made between 1999 and 2000, this quilt has a distinctly festive look with poinsettias, holly, ribbons, and bells. The appliqué, embroidery, and beading are sewn by hand. Machine quilting completes the piece.

Margaret Docherty

FROGMORE, 92" x 92", by Zena Thorpe. Zena has tied exquisite bouquets with ribbons and used architectural designs, befitting a ceiling, to divide her central medallion and borders. PHOTO: PHOTOGRAPHER

Margaret Docherty

WELCOME TO MY DREAMS, 79½" x 86½", by Betty Ekern Suiter. Betty's quilts, which resemble those of the 1930s, will, no doubt, be seen in future generations as timeless beauties rather than reminiscent of one particular era.

Margaret Docherty

Although BIRDS 'N' ROSES has the basic elements of the old quilts, it deviates from the original order of design in several ways: the center of the medallion is asymmetrical, the swag and middle border have been replaced with dense appliqué, and it has an appliquéd outer border. It is a Garden Quilt by default, rather than a copy of an old version. Many modern quilters, such as Karen Kay Buckley, Zena Thorpe, Betty Ekern Suiter, Shoko Ferguson, and Keiko Miyauchi, are also making Garden Quilts of their own design.

Karen Kay Buckley was voted teacher of the year in 1997 by *Professional Quilter* magazine. An author of several books and maker of many award-winning quilts, she must hold the record number of cover quilts for *Quilter's Newsletter Magazine*. Karen professes to loving flowers and gardens but dislikes the practical aspect of weeding and digging. Instead, she delights quilters the world over with her fabric gardens. Karen Kay Buckley's quilt is shown on page 17.

Zena Thorpe, having had a quilt designated as a Masterpiece by the National Quilt Association, is a member of the Master Quilter Guild. She is well known for her detailed and colorful award-winning hand-appliquéd quilts. Born in England, Zena frequently uses English history as an inspiration for her eclectic themes.

FROGMORE is such a quilt, on page 18. The inspiration came from a heavily decorated ceiling at Frogmore, one of Queen Victoria's favorite houses, set in Windsor Great Park. In the 1790s, Queen Charlotte commissioned Mary Moser to paint a room in the house with garlands of flowers. It is the ceiling of this room that inspired Zena's quilt.

Betty Ekern Suiter, like Zena Thorpe, is a Master Quilter and makes one masterpiece award-winning quilt after another. With a background as a draftsman, and often inspired by intricate antique carpet designs, she designs astounding, flowing floral fantasies. She frequently dyes her own fabrics to obtain the exact shades she requires. Betty Ekern Suiter's quilt is shown on page 19.

Shoko Ferguson first became interested in quilts in 1986 when her mother-in-law showed her some family heirlooms. After moving to Maryland from Japan in 1991, she began piecing scrap quilts and soon developed a taste for appliqué.

Shoko also loves miniature quilts and turned a well-known 1930s Garden Quilt into a design of her own making. At 41¼" square, her award-winning quilt MY BLUE GARDEN, page 21, is less than half the size of the original quilt made by Josephine Emma Craig.

Keiko Miyauchi's award-winning quilts often favor a floral theme. BLUE EARTH WITH WATER AND FLOWERS, page 22, is one of her most beautiful. This delectable and perfectly symmetrical quilt has been a great favorite at many quilt shows. The central medallion is packed with colorful flowers and butterflies, which are repeated in the wide corner units.

MY BLUE GARDEN, 41¼" x 41¼", by Shoko Ferguson. Shoko has set her tiny Garden Quilt, edged with stuffed feathered quilting, diagonally into a blue background edged with a scalloped flower border.

Margaret Docherty

BLUE EARTH WITH WATER AND FLOWERS, 85" x 76", by Keiko Miyauchi. A delicate ring of small circles acts as a circular border and is repeated at the edge of the quilt to form a scalloped frame. The wide, plain blue border acts as a perfect showcase for stuffed quilting.

Margaret Docherty

CHAPTER 2

Garden Quilt Design

Margaret Docherty

This section is for quilters who would like to design their own version of a Garden Quilt. The information may also be useful for those wanting to use large circular areas in a quilt design, with or without the Garden Quilt appliqué. Large circular pieces are more complicated to design than 12" blocks, but with the right equipment, which is not expensive or complex, and a little patience, almost anything can be achieved.

Drafting Supplies

✿ **Tracing paper.** Rolls of strong tracing paper are available from drafting supply outlets. Wide paper of a good length will allow most of the central medallion to be drawn out in full. Sheets of tracing paper stuck together with masking tape will suffice if a roll is not available. Scraps of tracing paper are also needed for tracing individual motifs.

✿ **Yardstick compass.** Available at quilting or drafting supply shops.

✿ **Mechanical lead pencil.** The endlessly sharp point is so helpful.

✿ **Eraser**

✿ **Protractor**

Thoughts on Design

In designing your quilt, ask yourself how long it will take to make. The central medallion does not need to be packed with flowers. A looser design or one with large, rather than small, floral motifs is just as effective and less time-consuming to sew. A simpler concept is also easier to design.

The continuity of the design is important. A quilt with a central medallion of roses and lilies will not look good with a border of primroses and violets. The flowers in the borders do not all need to be identical to those in the center, but a degree of continuity is necessary for a balanced design.

Keep the middle border simple. The swag is the master element of this border, and too many flowers only serve as a distraction.

Consider the complexity of the flowers. Complex shapes, such as roses, will take time to sew. Think before placing dozens of them in the design. If a sketched flower looks rather complicated, simplify the lines a little to make the appliqué easier. Some embellishment with embroidery and ink will help to add any missing details to the fabric flower.

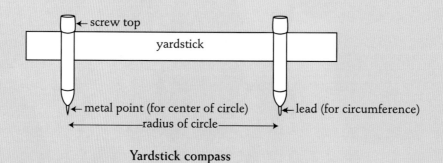

← screw top

yardstick

← metal point (for center of circle)

←lead (for circumference)

←——————radius of circle——————→

Yardstick compass

In a classic Garden Quilt the corner appliqué units square off the circle. The corner unit is wide at the corners and fades to nothing at the middle of each side of the quilt. Beyond this is a variable area of undecorated background fabric, an opportunity to show off fine quilting stitches.

As an example of the possible dimensions of a Garden Quilt, the central portion is contained within a circle 30" in diameter. A swag sitting half way between the inner and outer borders lies on a circle with a diameter of 52½". The outer circle has a diameter of 75". The length of each long, straight edge of the quilt is 75". A plain outer border, 7" wide, will give a finished quilt size of 89" square.

Master Pattern

Always draw at least a quarter of the pattern for the center area, preferably a half. If not, you may end up with areas that are devoid of appliqué or, worse still, that overlap when drawn out in full. Think of the design as a kaleidoscope. You never know what it will look like until all the sections have been joined.

Marking Guidelines

To begin drawing your master pattern, you will need a square of tracing paper, preferably the size of the whole center area. Draw the circle guidelines then divide them into four sections. This can be done easily by placing the tracing paper on a large cutting mat and using the squared grid on the mat to create the horizontal and vertical lines. Use the 45-degree line on the mat to further divide the circles into eight sections.

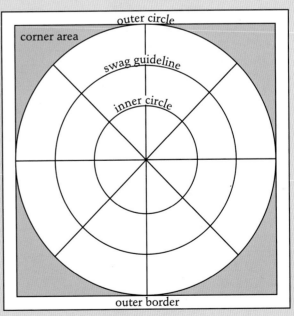

Design guidelines

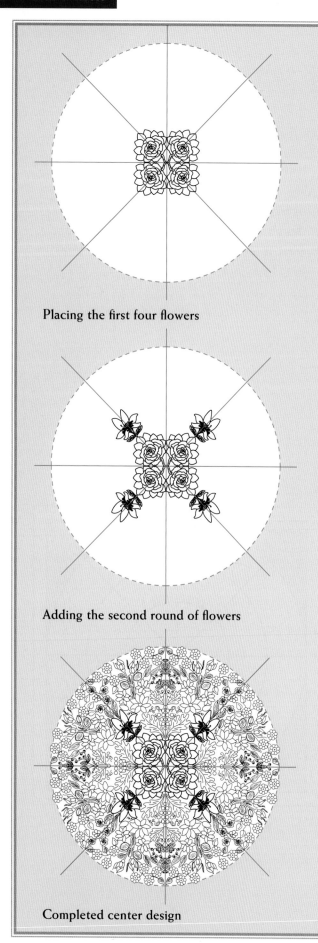

Placing the first four flowers

Adding the second round of flowers

Completed center design

Center Area Design

Start designing in the center area. The design may not reach the circle, or it may overshoot it. It is not a good idea to design with the constriction that you must not overstep the circle you have drawn, or again, that you must design right up to it. When complete, if the center design is smaller or larger than planned, it will then be no problem to adjust the size of the borders.

Have the center point of the circle clearly marked. Erasing unsuccessful attempts at design may wipe out guidelines, so being able to locate the center of the circle is useful when drawing them in again.

Fit four roses snugly into the very center, as follows: Trace a rose onto a scrap of tracing paper. Place the scrap rose under the master pattern where you want it and trace the rose onto the master pattern. Then place the scrap rose on top of the master pattern and realign it with the master rose. Trace the adjacent guidelines onto the scrap rose.

Place the scrap rose under the master pattern again, and trace the other three roses onto the master pattern. Aligning the guidelines on the scrap with those on the master pattern ensures that each rose will be positioned the same in each section. Turn the scrap rose over to produce the two reverse images—diagonally opposite roses are the same and adjacent ones are reverse images.

Next, position a large flower on each of the 45-degree section lines. The original

Garden Quilts have a lily-like flower in this position. To try out your own flower design, place a scrap of tracing paper over the 45-degree line on the master pattern and draw your flower on the scrap where you think it should lie. When the shape of the flower is satisfactory and the positioning suitable, add landmarks, such as the edges of roses and section guidelines, to the scrap flower. Place the scrap flower underneath the master pattern, align the landmarks, and trace the flower onto the master pattern.

Add large leaves next, eight in all, set in four pairs: Draw two scrap leaves, one a reverse image, and lay them over the master pattern. Move the leaves around until their positions are satisfactory. As before, trace landmarks from the master pattern onto the scrap paper around the leaves. Place the scraps underneath the master pattern, align the landmarks, and trace the leaves onto the master pattern.

Continue to work with scrap tracings like this throughout the remainder of the designing process. Fill in any gaps in the center medallion with rosebuds, grapes, small leaves, floral sprays, and vine tendrils. Buds can touch or project just beyond the perimeter of the inner circle.

Swag Border Design

Put the completed center-area master pattern aside and use a new, large piece of tracing paper to make a master pattern for the swag border. You need only a quarter of the swag design for the master pattern.

Align a straight edge of the tracing paper along one end of a cutting mat and attach the paper firmly with masking tape. Set the compass radius at 15" and draw the inner arc, approximately one-fourth of a circle. Reset the radius to 27" and draw another quarter arc to represent the placement line for the swag. Draw another quarter arc with a radius of 37½" for the outer circle.

There are sixteen swag loops in the swag border. That's four loops per quarter arc, so divide the quarter arc into eight sections. This can be done using a protractor (the angle is 11¼ degrees). Directions for two different swag border designs follow.

Symmetrical swag with ribbons. Using a scrap tracing as described previously, trace a rose onto the quarter master pattern.

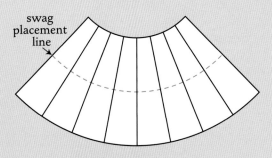

swag placement line

Quarter-circle sections

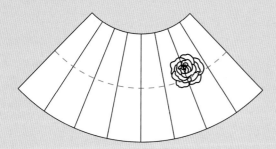

Rose placement

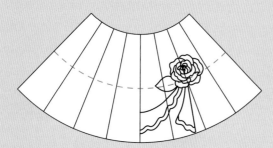

Half swag and ribbon

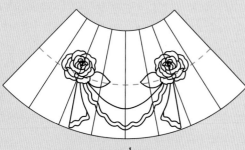

swag loop

swag quarter

Symmetrical swag with ribbons

Draw half of a swag between the rose and the adjacent guideline. Draw a ribbon on the same side of the rose as the drawn swag. Trace the rose, swag, ribbon, and guidelines onto a tracing paper scrap.

Turn the scrap over to create a reverse image, and place it underneath the master pattern in the adjacent section. Match the landmarks, paying particular attention to the central frill, and complete the swag and the adjacent rose and ribbon. Continue adding swag sections to the master pattern.

Continuous swag. In this design, the swag loop is not symmetrical. It is a continuous pattern repeated in the sections without being reversed (see figures on page 29). Be sure that the swag fits evenly across the first and last sections of the quarter master pattern and that it does not droop awkwardly on one side.

On the outer edge of the swag, traditional Garden Quilts have appliquéd designs, alternating a flower with a bird—eight birds and eight flowers in total.

Corner-Area Design

To make a master corner pattern, trace the outer arc from the swag pattern onto a new, large piece of tracing paper. This arc is the inner edge of the corner unit. Draw straight lines along two sides of the arc to meet at a 90-degree angle, to represent the corner of the quilt. Draw a guideline from the corner to meet the center of the arc, dividing the pattern in half. Flatten the curve of the arc slightly where it touches the sides of the corner unit.

The design across the corner is symmetrical, so you need work on only one half of the corner. The pattern can be transferred to the other half of the corner unit once the design is complete.

Using a scrap rose as before, position a rose in the corner of the master pattern. To add a leaf to the rose, position a blank scrap of tracing paper on the master pattern and draw the leaf on the scrap where you think it should be positioned. When the leaf shape is satisfactory and the positioning suitable, add landmarks, such as the straight lines and the edges of the rose, to the scrap.

Place the scrap leaf underneath the master pattern, align the landmarks and trace the leaf onto the master pattern. Continue adding leaves around the rose as desired. Add large flowers across the corner area that are roughly positioned in a straight line.

Continue to use scrap tracings to try out each flower and leaf before adding it to the master pattern. Aim to have the foliage touching the edge of the inner circle.

Connect the flowers with stems. Continue the stem line, curving it slightly, into the narrow area of the corner unit. Fill in the narrow area with grapes and grape leaves. In traditional Garden Quilts, the center of the corner has a bunch of grapes with mirror-image symmetry.

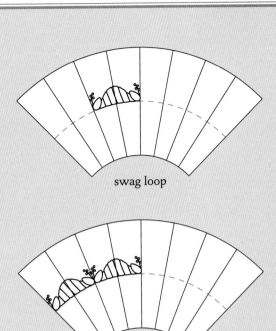

swag loop

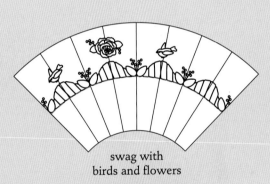

swag section

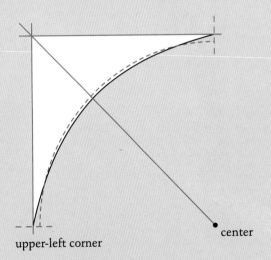

swag with
birds and flowers

Continuous swag

upper-left corner

center

Guidelines for corner unit

Margaret Docherty

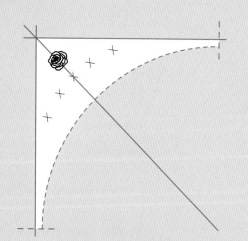

The Xs show where to place the large flowers.

Fill in the areas around the large flowers with small flowers that were used previously in the center medallion. Add leaves as necessary to fill in the gaps.

When you are happy with the design, fold the master pattern in half on the diagonal and transfer the reverse image to the other half of the corner area.

Once all the master patterns are complete, fit them together to see how they look before marking the background fabric.

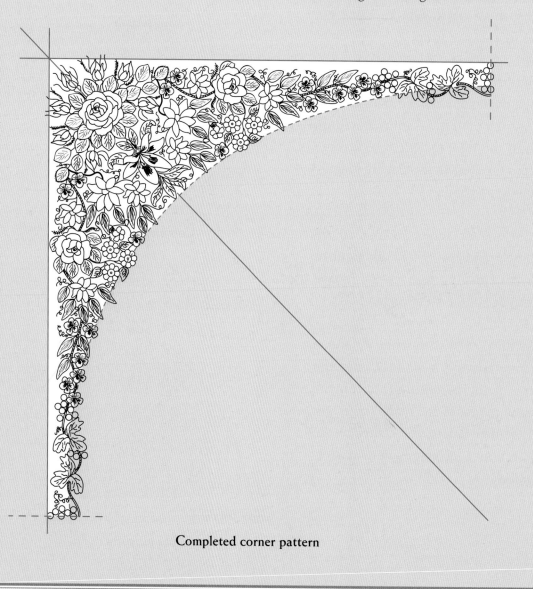

Completed corner pattern

CHAPTER 3

Flora, Fauna and Fabric

Margaret Docherty

The Flowers

BIRDS 'N' ROSES was named not only for its roses, but also for its primroses. The circular border comprises sixteen rosettes, alternating polyanthus and auriculas, both members of the primula family. Two overlapping rosettes of auriculas are at the very center of the medallion. Auriculas appear again in the border, in a different setting. In total, there are 463 auricula flowers, each comprising eight petals and a center. This is 4,167 appliqué pieces, not counting the polyanthus! A certain degree of enthusiasm about the flower is needed to proceed, and for those who are not ardent admirers of the auricula, alternate patterns are provided on pages 104–125.

Primula auricula

The history of the auricula is every bit as interesting as the history of quiltmaking, and as one picture is worth more than a thousand words, several pictures of flowers grown by members of the Auricula Society in the United Kingdom are included.

Auricula Dilly Dilly

PHOTO: KEITH LEEMING

Nowadays, we consider a florist to be a person who sells flowers. This is a fairly recent meaning of the word. The original meaning for "florist" was a gardener who grew and raised plants to agreed standards. Auriculas have been known as florist flowers for centuries.

From the early seventeenth century, shows were held for florist flowers including auriculas. Records suggest that the early florist was exclusively male, and the shows, which were held at inns, included a feast and a fair degree of insobriety. A regular boys night out! The arrival on the scene of female florists some centuries later may account for the respectability of the societies today.

Auricula Rajah

PHOTO: KEITH LEEMING

There became an accepted way to display auriculas in competition for, what would have been at the time, not inconsiderable sums of prize money. The plants were set in terra cotta pots and displayed against a black backcloth, which set off the exotic colors to perfection. The showcase was called an "auricula theatre," because it resembled a small stage.

Auriculas were recognized as far back as 1597. They are descended from two types of primula found in the European Alps. The modern florist auricula is a man-made hybrid, and there are several varieties of them, namely striped, edged, Alpine, self, and double.

The first auriculas to create a stir were striped. With a little imagination, one or two of the auriculas in BIRDS 'N' ROSES might be classed as striped. These auriculas lost popularity as new hybrids appeared.

How exotic the new edged auriculas were, in colors of gray, white, or green. I particularly wanted to depict in my quilt a variety called Margaret Martin, a gray-edged auricula, because this was my mother's maiden name. The representation of edged auriculas in fabric was not good, however. Surrounded by green rosettes on a pale cream background, exotic became drab.

More colorful varieties appeared, known as Alpine auriculas. The petals, in bright hues, are dark at the center and fade to a paler color at the rim. The center, or ground, is pale cream or deep yellow-gold in a florist flower.

There is also a type of florist auricula called a "self." The outer part of the petals is uniform in color and therefore the easiest to copy in fabric.

Auricula Stripe Spokey

PHOTO: KEITH LEEMING

Edged Auricula Margaret Martin

PHOTO: KEITH LEEMING

Edged Auricula Prague

PHOTO: KEITH LEEMING

Alpine Auricula Bilbo Baggins

PHOTO: KEITH LEEMING

Margaret Docherty

Polyanthus Pacific Giant

PHOTO: BRIAN DOCHERTY

Primula vulgaris

This large-flowered hybrid is a popular winter bedding plant in the United Kingdom. It is very hardy and creates a bright splash of garden color throughout the winter months when little else is growing. A few stray yellow polyanthus fill in the gaps around the rosettes of auriculas in the center area of the quilt as well as alternating with auriculas in the circular border.

Claude Monet Rose

PHOTO: THOMPSON AND MORGAN

Roses

After the primulas in the center of the medallion come the roses. Seasonally, the roses follow the primulas. The roses in BIRDS 'N' ROSES are of no particular named variety. Shades of yellow, pink, red, apricot, orange, and maroon are used to suggest petals at varying stages of opening. The finished effect is a variegated or striped rose. They are roughly the shape of an old rose, somewhere between a cabbage rose and a bourbon rose.

Claude Monet, a new hybrid tea rose introduced since BIRDS 'N' ROSES was completed, has petals ideal for a quilter. A red-and-yellow, tie-dye fabric would be perfect for this rose.

Clematis Lavender Green

PHOTO: KEITH LEEMING

Clematis

After the roses in the center of the medallion, surrounded by rose foliage and buds, come the clematis. According to the species and variety, clematis flower all year. Clematis could be in bloom at the same time as a primula or rose or even later in the gardening year. This shrub is the most popular climber in British gardens, and fanciers claim it to be the most exotic climbing shrub available to gardeners. It certainly is the most versatile.

The clematis comes in all colors, shapes, and sizes. It is difficult to find a true blue clematis. Most varieties have a degree of purple or lilac.

Clematis Florida Sieboldii is a white variety with bold purple staminodes. This flower would look fabulous represented in fabric and embroidery on a dark background. However, with the cream background used for BIRDS 'N' ROSES, the flower would have faded into oblivion, leaving what would appear as a gap in the appliqué when viewed from a distance. Yellow varieties were also rejected for the same reason. A palette of purple, blue, pink, and maroon was used for the clematis flowers.

Clematis Anna Louise

PHOTO: JULIE TAYLOR

Geranium

The varieties of flowers so far described are well known and prestigious. Devotees of auriculas, roses, and clematis are members of societies named for their favorite flower worldwide. Not so the final floral offering in BIRDS 'N' ROSES—the geranium.

The small yellow through orange, pink, and red flowers in the quilt cannot be botanically identified. They started life as a small purple flower from the Geranium family. This is not the popular large-headed red or pink geranium, which is actually a Pelargonium, but a modest flower also known as Cranesbill. It comes in all shades of pink, blue, purple, or white, but never orange and yellow!

Following a ring of blue and purple clematis in the center of the medallion, a warmer color was needed for the next ring of flowers, hence some compromise between botanical accuracy and color choice was called for. This flower pattern is used again in the corner areas. A larger version of the flower was selected for the floral motifs in the outer border. These flowers have more realistic colors of pink and plum.

The same flowers (primula, rose, clematis, and geranium) are used throughout the quilt. The addition of small red berries to the corner areas is the only deviation from the original flowers in the center of the medallion.

Geranium

PHOTO: JULIE TAYLOR

European Robin

PHOTO: SUE TRANTER

Blue Tit

PHOTO: SUE TRANTER

The Birds

The pattern is the same for all the birds but different fabrics were used to depict different species. All the birds are regular visitors to English gardens. There are sixteen birds in the center area, representing eight different species.

Robin

The North American robin is a large, dramatic dark gray bird with a red breast—not so the European robin. He is a small, downy, soft olive-brown bird, only 5½" long, with an orange-red breast that fades into buff at its lower end. He puffs up his chest in the most appealing and arrogant fashion. Young robins have speckled breasts. The red color comes with maturity.

The robin is regularly voted the favorite British bird, and, since 1961, it was adopted as the national bird. His popularity comes not only for his color, but also for his personality. He is said to be a friendly bird, regularly seen perching on garden spades. He will follow you around the garden, just a few paces behind. Actually, he is waiting for you to turn over some soil, exposing an earthworm, his favorite dinner.

He is also a notoriously aggressive little chap and very territorial. Robins will not tolerate each other in gardens, fighting quite dramatically to obtain "top-dog" status and access to the food supply. They have a tendency to nest in the most unlikely places and are famous for taking over your garden shed during the breeding season.

Blue Tit

This is a pretty bird with yellow, white, blue, and green plumage, a really cute little fellow, 4½" long. Peanuts are his favorite food. The blue tit is the acrobat at the bird feeder and quite intelligent. He is always the first to work out how to get food from new containers, and hanging upside down to feed is no problem for him. Milk delivered to the doorstep in bottles with tin-foil caps has long been the target of blue tit activity. They peck through the caps to get at the milk.

Song Thrush

The British song thrush, at 9" long, is larger than the other birds depicted in Birds 'n' Roses. He is not such a glamorous chap, being drab brown with a speckled breast. He is most often seen hopping across a lawn, watching the ground as he moves, with his head turned sideways. It is said his hopping mimics the sound of rain, and unsuspecting earthworms come to the surface in response, only to be gobbled up.

A song thrush is named for his voice, which is pure music. This is not the only sound he makes. As an insectivorous bird, he loves snails, and the regular sound of a thrush cracking a snail shell on a stone (his anvil) tells you he is there, even if you can't see him.

Song Thrush

Greenfinch

One of the three finches on the quilt, this chap is about 6" long with green and yellow plumage. He is not quite as green as he appears on the quilt, and the yellow bars on his wings are missing. This is probably the least recognizable bird on the quilt.

He has a thick heavy beak adept at cracking seed, and he just loves black sunflower seed. He does not visit the bird feeder alone. A whole flock descends, feeds, and departs—always in a hurry—with a whirring of wings when startled, which upsets all the other birds.

Greenfinch

Chaffinch

The chaffinch is our second most common British bird. It is 6" long, the same size as its cousin, the greenfinch. He can be found in parks and suburban gardens but is more a resident of the countryside.

The males and females have different coloring, the female being drabber than the male. Two male birds are depicted on Birds 'n' Roses. It is a pretty bird with a blue head, pink chest and face, chestnut back, and dark brown wings with white markings.

The chaffinch is not as agile as the greenfinch or blue tit. He does not feed from seed holders hanging from trees but hops around on the ground below the feeders and collects seed as it falls to the ground.

Chaffinch

Margaret Docherty

Bullfinch

PHOTO: SUE TRANTER

Bullfinch

Seeing this handsome chap coming to the bird feeder never fails to brighten up the dreariest day. He is 5¾" long, with a stunning bright rose pink breast and black cap. The female has the same black cap but a dull gray-beige breast. They always come to feed together, and it is thought that they mate for life.

Fruit growers detest them, because they are prone to eat buds from fruit trees when other food is scarce. They also relish sunflower seeds and can feed from seed holders like greenfinches.

Yellowhammer

The yellowhammer, especially the male whose colors are brighter than the female's, has a yellow, slightly speckled breast and a bright yellow head. The wings and tail are brown with chestnut highlights. He is well known for his instantly recognizable song, "A-little-bit-of-bread-and-no-cheese."

This bird is a bunting, about 6½" long. He lives on farmland and is a seedeater. Although a fairly common bird, he is said to be too shy to come into gardens. He does visit rural gardens when the weather is bad and eats whatever seed is available on the ground.

Yellowhammer

PHOTO: SUE TRANTER

Tree Sparrow

PHOTO: SUE TRANTER

Tree Sparrow

The tree sparrow is 5½" long and has a chestnut head and a distinct black spot on his cheeks, which distinguishes him from the more common house sparrow. Tree sparrows move around in flocks, and a flock of them sitting on the bare branches of a magnolia tree in winter looks for all the world as if the tree has sprouted winter blossoms.

The Fabrics

A wide palette of fabrics was used for the appliqué in BIRDS 'N' ROSES. Choices were made from a large stash of fabrics, many of which were earmarked specifically for flowers and leaves. None of the appliqué pieces are painted. The challenge of finding just the right commercially produced fabric adds to the fun of fabric selection.

Hand-dyed fabrics used in the quilt were all produced commercially and carefully selected. Blotchy tie-dyes with patches of white showing through strong colors are ideal. A template can be arranged over a blotchy area to give the impression of light shining on a bird's wing or to depict different intensities of color on a flower petal.

As fabrics were auditioned for the flowers, it became obvious that pastel shades were of no use. The dark cream background of the center area and the wide-open space of the circular border made pastels disappear. The brightest or deepest shade from a possible palette appeared the most satisfactory choice every time.

Many of the fabrics selected, in a length of one-half yard or a fat quarter, are garish, but when reduced to six or seven small petals set in green foliage and a cream background, they lose some of the brashness and, in some cases, are quite realistic.

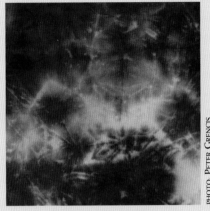

Blue tie-dye fabric

Auriculas with shading

Auricula

Initially, green and blue-gray were selected as colors for the auriculas. However, once transferred to fabric and set in a green rosette of leaves, the effect was lost. Exotic became drab.

Purples, reds, orange, maroon, and bright pink proved to be a pleasing compromise. These are also the colors of auriculas, but of a more common variety, the

Fabric selection for auriculas

Polyanthus on quilt

Alpine auricula, which is readily available for ordinary gardeners. The size of each individual petal for this group of flowers is very small, which is far too challenging to try to get the appearance of natural shading from light to dark in each petal. To add some depth and shading to the flowers, petals are grouped together. Several flowers are dark, while adjoining flowers are much lighter.

Polyanthus

These plants are available in all colors, and some are extremely vivid—a great splash of color in a winter garden. Possible fabrics for appliqué were held against real flowers. Beside the real thing, the less vivid fabrics appeared drab and uninteresting. Even the less intense shades of polyanthus, pale blues, pinks, and yellows, had a certain luminosity that made pastel fabrics appear drab.

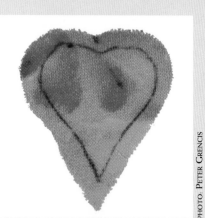

One flower petal

PHOTO. PETER GRENCIS

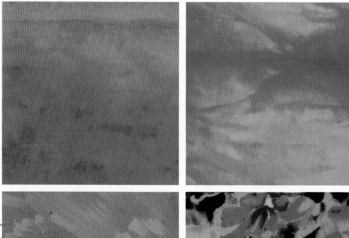

PHOTO. PETER GRENCIS

Fabric selection for polyanthus

Leaves

Each ring of flowers is set in a rosette of green leaves. The greens in the circular border are all different, Fussy cutting (described on page 60) naturally produced leaf markings for some. Ink lines produced leaf veins for others.

The same green fabrics, with some additions, were used for the auricula rosette background in the border. One set of polyanthus leaves was cut from a fabric covered in cabbages.

A range of green fabrics, from yellow through to blue-green with browns and reds, were used for the primula, rose, and clematis foliage.

Cabbage leaf rosette

PHOTO: PETER GRENCIS

Fabric selection for leaves

Leaves in the center area

Roses

The flowers in the quilt are variegated roses. A good hand dyer could produce a graduated batch of pink, orange, red, or yellow fabric that would allow for single-fabric roses to be made with enough variation in intensity of color to depict appropriate shading.

The multicolored roses were made from at least 30 different fabrics. The corner roses are all orange. Pink and orange were alternated in the center roses.

Foliage for the roses does not necessarily have to be green. Many roses have deep-red leaves. For the center area, a palette of red through yellow-green to blue-green was used for the leaves. Symmetry is obtained by making *mirror-image* motifs of the medallion in the same shades. In the corner areas, the leaves are mainly red.

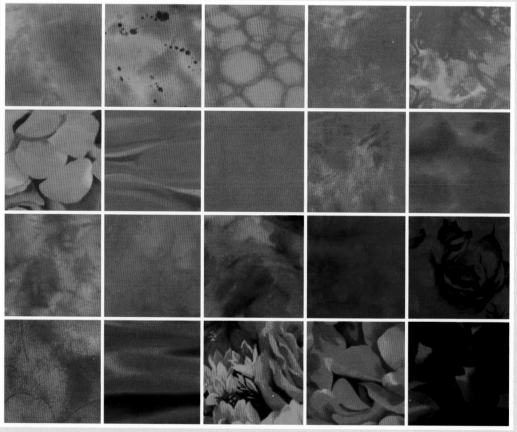

PHOTO: PETER GRENCIS

Fabric selection for roses

Margaret Docherty

Clematis

A palette of pink, purple, maroon, and blue was used for the clematis. The petals of the larger clematis are substantial in size, allowing more leeway with fabric selection than for the tiny primula flowers.

Some flowers have light-dark shading. Others have a stripe through the petal or a darker color at the center or petal edge. The clematis leaves are depicted in yellow through yellow-green to blue-green.

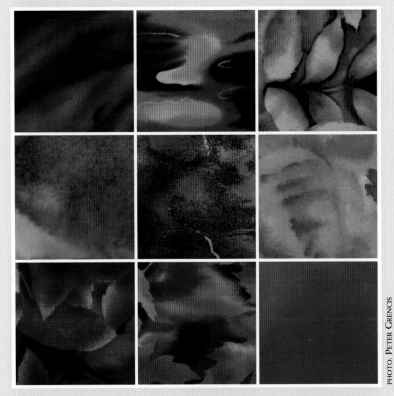

PHOTO: PETER GRENCIS

Fabric selection for clematis

Corner rose with red leaves

Clematis flower and leaves

Close-up of small flowers

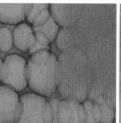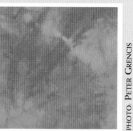

Fabric selection for small flowers

PHOTO. PETER GRENCIS

Close-up of berries

Close-up of blue loop

Small Flowers

The small flowers were shaded through yellow to orange, pink, and red in three fabrics.

Berries

Berries were done in a red-orange fabric and a red-purple fabric. They are so small that the only requisite for them is a strong color. Shading or a pattern in the fabric is not necessary.

Ribbons and Loops

The fabric used for the ribbons and loops was blue, mottled with dark and light shading. Appliqué pieces were cut with dark shading on the under curve of the loop and light on the top. The blue mottled fabric was one of three "staple" fabrics used in the quilt. It was also used for the binding.

The ugly burgundy rose fabric, another staple, was used for the clematis and all the small flowers in the border. It also provided the broderie perse (described on page 60) rosebuds in the border.

The third staple fabric was a yellow and pink floral, selected for the polyanthus. This fabric was used for two rosettes of polyanthus, several rose petals, rosebuds, and some of the small flowers.

PHOTO: PETER GRENCIS

Staple fabrics

Birds

Before selecting fabrics for birds, think about the general arrangement of their feathers. A fabric covered in an exotic, large feather print is seldom of any use for appliquéing a small bird, except, perhaps for the tail feathers. If a suitable fabric cannot be found, simple ink lines or fine embroidery, used sparingly, can be used to indicate feathers.

The most difficult part of the bird to portray realistically is the wing. Some birds, such as the chaffinch, have white bars on their wings. A brown fabric with white streaks is ideal for wings and tail.

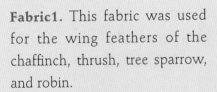

Close-up of small flowers in the border

Fabric1. This fabric was used for the wing feathers of the chaffinch, thrush, tree sparrow, and robin.

Fabrics 2 and 3. These were used in two colorways, one yellow-brown and the other green-brown, for the wings and tail of the yellowhammer and greenfinch.

Fabric 4. Breast feathers are fluffy. In this gray and taupe fabric, the leaves have white feathery edges. This fabric was used for the breast feathers of the tree sparrow.

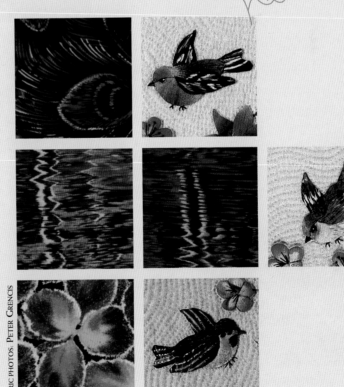

FABRIC PHOTOS: PETER GRENCIS

Margaret Docherty

Fabric 5. Yellowhammer. The breast was cut from this shaded, yellow, mottled fabric.

Fabric 6. Robin. A fabric with gray and red blotches was ideal to show the robin's breast feathers.

Fabric 7. Thrush. A fabric depicting a cornfield looks very like a thrush's speckled breast.

Fabric 8. Greenfinch. A green impressionistic leaf fabric yielded the right color for the breast.

Fabric 9. Blue tit. The white face, yellow breast, and blue head were cut as a unit from this fabric.

FABRIC PHOTOS: PETER GRENCIS

Embellishments

The yellowhammer's breast and head were enhanced with ink lines and straight stitch embroidery. Tail feathers are best marked with longitudinal lines, and back feathers run in horizontal rows. For a small bird, these rows can be suggested with short ink or embroidered lines running from head to tail.

Yellowhammer

CHAPTER 4

Appliqué and Embellishment

Margaret Docherty

Flora and Fauna Index

	Photo (page)	Description (page)	Fabric (page)	Pattern (page)
Flora				
Auricula	32–33	32, 51, 58	39	84, 96–99
Polyanthus	34	34, 49	40	85–86
Roses	34	34, 52–53	42	77–80,89 114–115, 118
Clematis	34–35	34, 54	43	81–82, 90–94
Geranium	35	35		96
Leaves	57	57	41	89–91
Small flowers	55	54	44	81–82, 91, 94
Berries	56	56	44	90–92, 94
Fauna				
Robin	36	36, 57	45–46	81–82
Blue Tit	36	36, 57	46	81–82
Song Thrush	37	37, 57	45–46	81–82
Greenfinch	37	37, 57	45–46	81–82
Chaffinch	37	37, 57	45	81–82
Bullfinch	38	38, 57	—	81–82
Yellowhammer	38	38, 57	45–46	81–82
Tree Sparrow	38	38, 57	45	81–82
Other				
Ribbons and loops	56	55–56, 70–71	44	96–99

This chapter is devoted to each individual flower, leaf, and bird, along with some appliqué and embellishment tips.

Appliqué Supplies

❧ **Templates.** Each template will be used many times, so take a little time at the outset of the project to make your templates as stencils. It is easier to draw inside a stencil than it is to draw round a small plastic template. Small templates are also easily mislaid. A stencil is less likely to disappear.

A medium thickness of template plastic is ideal. A heavyweight plastic does not lend itself to cutting small curves for appliqué. A very thin plastic may become distorted as the shape is being drawn on the fabric.

Devotees of freezer paper will not need templates, but remember, auditioning fabric for just the right shading in a leaf or petal is easier with a plastic template.

❧ **Starch.** Stiff fabric is easier to mark.

❧ **Fine sandpaper.** Use a sheet of fine sandpaper to hold the fabric steady while marking the appliqué shapes.

❧ **Fine-lead pencil.** A mechanical lead pencil (0.7mm) is ideal for marking fabric. Water-soluble mechanical lead pencils are available for quilters.

❧ **Small pair of scissors.** Small scissors are ideal for cutting small appliqué pieces.

❧ **Fray retardant.** Before stitching, treat concave curves with fray retardant applied with a small paintbrush.

Polyanthus Rosettes
Appliqué Tips

Patterns are provided for flowers with five or six petals (pages 85–86). The basic shape of the petal is the same for both flowers. An alternative symmetrical auricula rosette for the center of the quilt is given on page 104. The polyanthus and auriculas are time consuming to stitch, so simpler alternatives are provided. A simpler center is given on pages 105–112. There is a swag to replace the auricula border on page 113. The optional outer border features auriculas. This border is not necessary for a classic Garden quilt.

To keep the light quilt background from showing between the flowers, make a green background for each rosette, as follows: From a template, cut the shape outlined by the broken line on the rosette pattern (page 84), and cut a patch of green fabric similar to or the same as the fabric used for the leaves. Appliqué the green background shape to the quilt background then cut away the quilt background from behind the green shape, leaving a ¼" seam allowance.

Mark the flower petals on the green shape. Appliqué the leaves in place. The numbering on the leaves is the suggested order for appliquéing them. Apply the flower petals, one flower at a time. The circled number shows the appliqué order for the flowers. There is much overlapping of the pieces, so try to ensure that the stitches go through all the fabric layers. Also check that the flower petals cover all the raw edges of the appliquéd leaves before stitching the petals to the background.

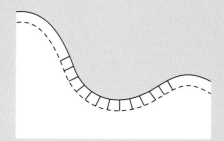

Clip all concave curves.

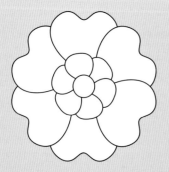

Polyanthus with alternate center

Pink polyanthus with a
different center

Treat the curved area in the center of the outer edge of each petal with fabric fray retardant and clip the curved seam allowance before stitching it down.

An alternative fabric center for the polyanthus flowers is used in two of the rosettes. The flower center is applied with fusible webbing and buttonhole stitched around the edges, as follows: Appliqué the petals to the background. Trace the flower center template onto the non-adhesive side of the fusible. (Remember, this method produces a reverse image the same as freezer paper, so turn your pattern over before tracing.) Rough-cut the shape and iron the sticky side to the selected fabric. Cut the fabric and fusible shape out carefully on the line. Remove the adhesive paper, exposing the second adhesive side of the fusible, and iron the shape to the center of the already appliquéd petals.

Add a scant ³⁄₁₆" turn-under allowance to fabric pieces as you cut. Leave a wider turning (¼") for an allowance that will be covered by another piece of appliqué. This wider allowance will provide a little leeway for overlapping if the pieces are not quite accurately positioned and stitched.

Embellishments

Using permanent marking pens in a variety of colors, mark veins on the edges of the petals. Embroider simple rings of French knots around the centers. Alternatively, embroider a small ring in outline stitch at the center of each flower. Use a fine thread to fill in the circle with French knots.

Embellishing Polyanthus

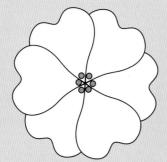

a. Ring of French knots

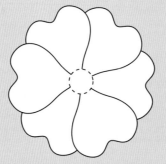

b. Outline-stitched center

c. Inked petal edges

Auricula Rosettes
Appliqué Tips

From a template the shape of the broken line shown on the rosette pattern (page 84), cut a patch of green fabric similar to, or the same as, the fabric used for the leaves. Appliqué this shape to the background fabric and cut away the background behind it, leaving a ¼" seam allowance.

Apply the leaves to the background fabric and the green shape. A few leaves appear folded. The pattern indicates two appliqué pieces for these folded leaves, and it is recommended that a lighter colored fabric be used for the folded edge of the leaf.

The flowers all have eight petals. A little variety in size and shape of the flowers will appear more natural than totally identical flowers. Apply the eight petals, overlapping different petals in the flowers so they don't all look the same. Where the appliqué pieces overlap, try to take the appliqué stitch through all the fabric layers.

There is a starred area on the pattern, at the base of leaf 7. This is a tricky area because, if the adjoining flowers do not meet, a raw leaf edge will show. Pay particular attention to this area, or alternatively, do not leave a raw edge at this spot. Instead, turn the allowance under and appliqué it to the background fabric.

The template given on this page for the petal is extra wide at the inner edge. Take a small tuck in the fabric at that edge and hold it in place with small basting stitches. The tuck will give the flowers a dimensional appearance.

Three different sizes of circles were used for the auricula flower centers, ⅝", ¹¹⁄₁₆", and ¾". If the flower petals are not accurately placed, use a larger center to cover any raw edges.

EMBELLISHING AURICULAS

a. Outline-stitched center

b. Inked center

c. French knots and inked edges

d. Inked petal veins

Auricula petal pattern

Rose sepals

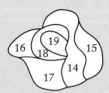

Center rose unit

Whole rose
(Full-sized pattern on page 77.)

Embellishments

As shown on page 51, use a stem-stitch to embroider a small circle around the center of the flower. Lightly shade the area inside the embroidered circle with a brown permanent-ink fabric pen. Use a light shade of thread to embroider French knots in the center of the flower on the inked area. Lightly ink the edges of the circular center and around the ring of embroidery. Also mark a ring of lines on the petals where they join the center of the flower.

Rose Flowers
Appliqué Tips

The roses in the center area have sepals attached. Apply the sepals to the background fabric before adding the rose. The rose stems vary in shape and length.

The central portion of the rose (appliqué pieces 14 to 19) is small. It is easier to piece these small shapes together and appliqué them to the rest of the rose as a unit. To ensure that each piece of the center rose unit is attached to the background, sew a small running stitch down the seam lines of the unit, taking the stitching through all the fabric layers.

Inking details on rose

PHOTO: PETER GRENCIS

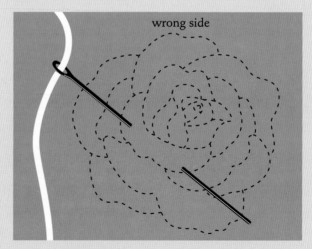

wrong side

Stuff flowers from the wrong side.

Margaret Docherty

Embellishments

Using a brown permanent-ink pen, draw veins on the petals. To add dimension to the roses, stuff some of the petals: Working from the reverse side of the quilt, use a trapunto needle and trapunto yarn of your choice. Insert the trapunto needle into one side of the petal and exit at the opposite side. Pull the yarn through until the tail is flush with the fabric at the entry hole. Put a little tension on the yarn and cut it where it exits the fabric. Reinsert the needle in either hole and use it to push the yarn to one side. Repeat until the petal is firmly stuffed but not so firm as to distort the surrounding fabric. Use an ordinary sewing needle to scratch the fabric fibers around the holes back in place. (A trapunto needle has a blunt end that will not tear the fabric fibers if used carefully.)

Do not stuff the petals until the rose and surrounding appliqué have been pressed. Do not stuff all the petals. This will give a disproportionate heaviness to the area of the quilt where the roses lie.

Consider using broderie perse for the whole rose or even just the center part. There are many fabrics on the market today, for quilting and drapery, that have roses printed on them.

Rosebuds and Leaves
Appliqué Tips

Use a red, orange, or pink fabric for pattern pieces 1 and 2 of the rosebud. Use a huge variety of color and fabric for the leaves. Try fussy cutting some and inking veins on others. The individual leaf shapes are simple to appliqué.

Embellishments

Add fronds to the rose buds with ink or embroidery. Stuff petal pieces 1 and 2. Ink leaf veins and hairs on the edges of the rose leaves. Embroider leaf stems in outline stitch.

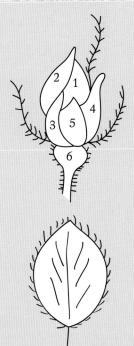

Embellishing rosebuds and leaves

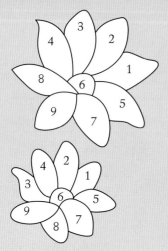

Clematis flowers
(Full-sized patterns on page 90.)

Ink lines on petals

Inked veins and
embroidered tendrils

Clematis Flowers
Appliqué Tips

There are two sizes of clematis flower. The numbering on the petals is the suggested order of appliqué. For the leaves, use a full range of green, yellow, and red fabrics.

Embellishments

Draw petal veins down the length of each petal for the clematis, rather than the short lines used at the outer edge of the rose petals. Use a trapunto needle and yarn to stuff the circular center patch. Embroider straight stitches over the center stuffed area. Work stems in a textured satin stitch. The stems of the large clematis can be appliquéd.

Clematis plants are climbing shrubs. They use tendrils to cling to trellises, poles, other plants, and anything they possibly can. Use an outline or stem stitch to embroider tendrils liberally on the outer reaches of the leaf stems.

Small Flowers
Appliqué Tips

There are three sizes for this flower. Small and medium ones are used in the center and corners of the quilt. The large size, in a different color, is used in the outer border.

Embellishments

Ink veins on the petals. Press all the flowers then use a trapunto needle and yarn to stuff them. Proceed as described in the instructions for embellishing roses on page 53. Embellish the flowers with embroidery after the stuffing is in place. Use a deep-purple, silk embroidery thread and sew straight stitches on some flowers and straight stitches with French knots at the ends to depict stamens on others.

Stems and Loops
Appliqué Tips

There are four rounds of ribbons and loops in Birds 'n' Roses. The first round outlines the center area of the medallion. The second round outlines the circular border. The third and fourth rounds outline the outer border.

The ribbon loops, each comprised of two parts, lie underneath a bias strip ³⁄₁₆" wide. When cutting strips on the bias, it is preferable to cut the total required length all at the same time. Make it the task for the day to cut all the bias strips.

Use your method of choice to prepare the bias strips. For Birds 'n' Roses, the following method was used: Starch the fabric. Mark two stitching lines, ³⁄₁₆" apart, across the full width of the fabric on the bias (at a 45 degree angle to the straight grain). A mechanical lead pencil is an ideal marker. Mark a seam allowance of ¼" on either side of the stitching lines. Continue marking strips until the total length of the marked strips equals the total length of bias needed. Cut the bias strips with a rotary cutter. The strips will be ⅞" wide (⅜" finished width, plus two ¼" turn-under allowances, equals ⅞".

Join the bias strips together, end to end, by hand or machine to make one continuous strip. Press the seam allowances between the strips open.

To appliqué the bias strip, sew the inner concave edge first, stitching just inside the pencil line so the marking is hidden in the allowance. Finger press the fold line as you progress along the strip.

After you have sewn the bias strip to the background, fold the strip back to expose the underside and trim away the excess allowance. On the unstitched edge, trim the turn-under allowance to approximately ³⁄₁₆" and proceed to turn, finger press, and stitch the second side of the bias strip to the background (see page 56).

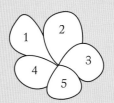

Small flower

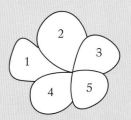

Medium flower

Large flower

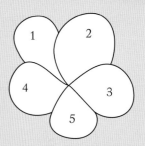

Inked and embroidered small flower

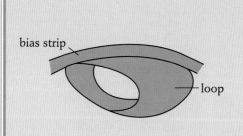

bias strip

loop

Ribbon loop

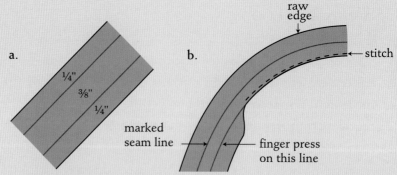

a.

¼"

⅜"

¼"

marked
seam line

Cutting and sewing a bias strip

b.

raw
edge

stitch

finger press
on this line

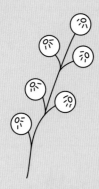

Embellished berries

Berries

Appliqué Tips

The corner appliqué areas contain the same flowers and leaves as the center, with the addition of small red berries and some tiny leaves. A standard paper hole punch was used to provide templates for the berries.

It is extremely difficult to remove the papers from such small appliqué pieces and still keep a reasonably shaped circle. As an alternative, you can substitute fewer, larger berries.

To construct the berries, cut circles from firm paper. Old greetings cards are ideal for this purpose. Polyester templates can also be used. (Polyester templates can withstand ironing.) Lightly starch the fabric to contain fraying. Add a generous seam allowance, about ½", to the berry. Sew basting stitches around the edge of the fabric circle. Fit the fabric over the template and draw up the stitches to pull the allowance to the back. If the circle is not perfect, put in another row of stitches closer to the outer edge of the circle and gather tightly again. Tie off the threads. Starch the berry well and press firmly. Cut the gathering stitches and ease the fabric circle off the template. Starch helps the berry to keep a good shape.

Embellishments

Join the berries together with a stem stitch worked in brown or green embroidery thread. Ink a small dot at one edge of the berry with a few small lines coming from the dot in a circular pattern. A little embellishment on a berry can help to camouflage a none-too-perfect circle.

Embellished small leaf

Small Leaves
Appliqué Tips and Embellishments

Small leaves were used to fill in gaps in the corner areas. Use a stem stitch to embroider the stems for the small leaves. Add leaf veins and leaf hairs in ink.

Birds
Embellishments

The birds are all constructed from the same pattern, so it is the embellishment that makes a bird. Embroider the beak in two parts by using a fine thread and a satin stitch. Embroider a suggestion of feet in fine thread and an outline stitch.

Embellished bird

Embroider the eye in a brown or gold outline stitch. Fill in the outline with a black satin stitch. Add a few stitches of white satin stitch on top of the black to highlight the eye.

If a plain fabric is used for the body, wings, and tail, add a few inked lines to the bird to suggest the direction of the feathers.

Border Flowers

The border is optional. It can be replaced by a 7" to 8" extension of the background fabric beyond the corner appliqué. The inner looped ribbon trimmed with bows and birds in the center will form a satisfactory edge to the quilt. Include an area of fancy quilting in the plain outer margins of the quilt.

Appliqué

The auriculas are featured again in the border but in a different arrangement. Each border has eight oval green "cushions," with six flowers arranged on each cushion. Forty-eight flower petals and six flower centers are needed for each cushion.

Mark both the outer and inner oval shapes. Cut out the center of the shape, leaving a ³⁄₁₆" turn-under allowance. Treat the allowance with a fray retardant and clip the edge generously. Turn the allowance to the wrong side and finger press it in place. If the allowance does not lie flat, turn it to the right side and clip again. Appliqué the inner oval first, taking care not to pucker the background fabric, then appliqué the outer edge of the cushion.

The small flower in the border is a larger version of those in the center and corner areas. Shades of burgundy, plum, and deep pink were used for these border flowers. Each small flower in the border units has two leaves. One is a reverse image of the other. The center floral motif has four leaves.

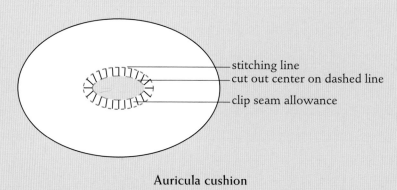

stitching line
cut out center on dashed line
clip seam allowance

Auricula cushion

Embellishment

Draw veins on the leaves and fronds on the rosebuds and stems with ink. There are rosebuds on either side of the small flowers in the border.

The rosebuds on the border of BIRDS 'N' ROSES were cut as motifs from a floral fabric, but the edges were turned under before stitching them to the background.

Embellished leaf and bud

SPECIAL CUTTING TECHNIQUES

Broderie perse. This term refers to motifs cut from a fabric print and appliquéd to a background. The technique has commonly been used to make floral quilts in which each flower and leaf is a printed design cut out from a selection of floral prints. Complex edges to the motif call for it to be appliquéd without the raw edges being turned under. Instead, a buttonhole stitch or blanket stitch is used to appliqué the raw edges to the background fabric. Modern-day quilters can machine appliqué the pieces by using a fabric stabilizer and a machine satin or other decorative stitch.

Broderie perse rose leaves

Fussy cutting. This method is similar to broderie perse. Instead of cutting out the whole motif, the shape the quilter requires is cut from a printed design on a pattern fabric. Fussy cutting can also refer to cutting a shape from a multicolored or mottled fabric with no particular design. By moving a template around the fabric, two colors or two intensities of color can be arranged in one shape. Most, if not all, of the appliqué pieces in BIRDS 'N' ROSES were cut this way.

As an example of fussy cutting, select a print fabric leaf. Place a leaf template on the print leaf so that the veins on the fabric leaf follow the shape of the template. When the appliqué piece is cut out and the edges turned under, the appliquéd leaf will appear as a smaller version of the print leaf.

Fussy-cutting leaves. Leaf shapes 1 and 2 were carefully planned, but shape 3 was not. The effect of leaf 3 will not be as pleasing.

Polyester templates. These were referred to in the text on how to make the berries (page 56). Circles made from firm, heat-resistant polyester in a variety of sizes are commercially available. They have a perfect shape, and because they are heat resistant, they can be pressed with a hot iron. Their great advantage is that they can be used many times, unlike paper or card-stock templates, which are usually destroyed when they are removed from the fabric.

CHAPTER 5

Birds 'n' Roses Quilt

Margaret Docherty

BIRDS 'N' ROSES, detail, 84" x 84", by the author. Full quilt shown on page 6.

Quilt Dimensions

- ❦ **Finished quilt before quilting** = 87" square

- ❦ **Center area** = 33" diameter (radius 16½")

- ❦ **Inner ribbon-and-loop ring** = 40" diameter (radius 20")

- ❦ **Outer ribbon-and-loop ring** = 58¾" diameter (radius 29⅜")

- ❦ **Finished quilt top without border** = 75" square

- ❦ **Finished border strips** = 6" x 87"

Margaret Docherty

Suggested Fabrics and Amounts

Yardages and Cutting			
Based on fabrics at least 40", except where noted.			
Fabric	**Location**	**Amount**	**Cut**
Pale cream	background	4¾ yards (42" wide)	2 panels 42" x 80"
Dark cream	background	4 yards (42" wide)	1 panel 45" x 42" 4 strips 8" x 90"
Mottled blue	ribbons, loops, binding	3½ yards	see Mottled Blue Cutting chart, page 64
Greens	leaves, stems, rose sepals, rosebuds	32 fat quarters	
Dark yellows, browns	clematis and rose leaves	2 fat quarters	
Bright yellow	small flowers, polyanthus flowers	1 fat quarter	
Pale yellow	rose petals	1 fat eighth	
Pale to dark yellows	auricula and polyanthus centers	scraps	
Orange-yellows	polyanthus flowers	2 fat quarters	
Reds	rose and clematis leaves, auricula flowers, berries	5 fat eighths	
Dark to light pinks and oranges	rose petals	6 fat eighths	
Bright oranges and pinks	small flowers	2 fat eighths	
Vibrant pinks and oranges	auricula flowers	6 fat eighths	
Purples, plums, burgundies, blues, lilacs	clematis and auricula flowers, small flowers, berries	21 fat eighths	
Backing		8⅜ yards	3 panels 33" x 95"

Mottled Blue Fabric		
Location	**Cut**	**Make**
Ribbon loops		
inner circle	32 loops and 32 reverse loops	
outer circle	32 loops and 32 reverse loops	
inner border edge	60 loops and 60 reverse loops	
outer border edge	68 loops and 68 reverse loops	
Bias ribbon strips		
inner circle	1 square 18" x 18"	continuous strip ⅞" x 157"
outer circle	1 square 18" x 18"	continuous strip ⅞" x 230"
inner border edge	1 square 22" x 22"	continuous strip ⅞" x 375"
outer border edge	1 square 23" x 23"	continuous strip ⅞" x 435"
Bias binding	1 square 32" x 32"	continuous strip 2½" x 360"

BACKGROUND FABRIC

Avoid constructing the quilt from one piece of 90"–95" fabric. It is difficult to appliqué onto such a large unwieldy area.

If using the same background fabric, 42" wide, for the whole quilt, still construct the center area separately to avoid a seam line in the center of it.

FABRIC MARKERS

Use a marker that is easily removed and not affected by an iron, because it may be necessary to press the center appliqué before progressing to the next area. Use a water-soluble marker sparingly so it can be removed with a minimum amount of water. Water-soluble markers are set by a hot iron and must be removed completely before pressing.

5. Cut out the center of the joined panels, leaving a ½" turn-under allowance. Clip the allowance then turn and finger press it to the wrong side of the fabric. Take care not to stretch the seam line. A little starch applied along the seam may be helpful.

6. Baste the turned-under allowance in place, taking care not to stretch the seam. Remove the basting stitches that marked the circle.

7. With both pieces right side up, lay the center panel on a firm surface, such as the floor. Smooth it flat and place the joined panels over it. Match the basted edge of the panels to the

circle on the center panel. Check that the grain of the center panel is correct and that the two large clematis flowers are centered.

8. Pin and baste the center panel in place. Check to see that the whole quilt top lies flat after basting.

9. Remove the basting stitches that mark the circle from the center panel. Firmly appliqué the center panel in place. On the back, cut away any excess fabric from the center panel.

10. Remove the basting stitches and gently press the turned-under allowances flat.

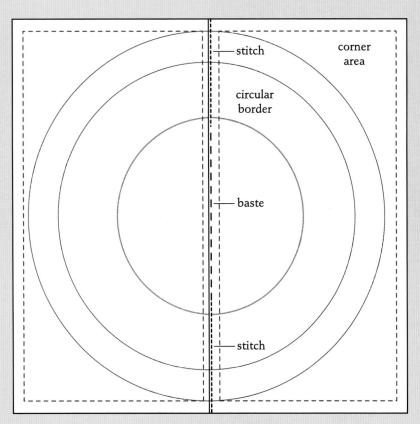

stitch

corner area

circular border

baste

stitch

Joining the panels

Ribbon and Loop Rings

1. On your master pattern, mark one ring with a radius of 20" and a second ring with a radius of 29⅜".

2. Align the circular border template over the appliquéd rosettes and the inner circle line. Mark the inner ribbon and loops on the background, matching the line running through the pattern to the seam line. Then mark the second ring of ribbon and loops.

3. Referring to the Mottled Blue Fabric chart (page 64), cut the number of fabric loops needed and make the bias ribbon strips.

4. Stitch the loops in place and cover the raw edges with the shortest bias strip.

PLACING LOOPS

There is one ribbon loop in every one sixty-fourth of the circle. The sector lines of the circle are marked on the pattern. The loops on the inner ribbon are closer together than those on the outer ribbon.

Outer Border

1. Three pattern sections are given for the border. From these pieces construct a master pattern half the length of one border plus the whole center flower motif. The pattern should measure 43½" from the outer seam line to the border center. Ensure that the paper for the pattern is wide enough to mark all the inner ribbon and loop trim.

2. Mark the center of the border fabric strip. Match the center of the pattern to the center of the fabric border and mark the pattern on the fabric with a water-soluble marker. Turn the pattern over and mark the reverse image on the second half of the border.

3. Refer to the following list to make templates and cut pieces for the outer border. Wait to appliqué the corner motif until the border corners have been mitered.

Each border strip:
8 green auricula cushions
8 sets of 6 auricula flowers
4 geranium flowers
4 reversed geranium flowers
9 leaves
9 reversed leaves
8 rosebuds and stems
8 reversed rosebuds and stems

4. Stitch the border strips to the four sides of the quilt and miter the corners. Finish appliquéing the corner motifs.

Ribbon and Loop Trim

1. Mark the ribbon and loop trim on the inner and outer edges of the border. Notice that the inner trim straddles the border seam.

2. Appliqué the loops to the border. The direction of the loops reverses at the middle of each border strip, and the two loops that meet in the middle form a bow. Appliqué a small oval shape over the center of each bow. Appliqué a bird on each side of the bows.

3. Carefully remove all markings from the quilt and press.

Quilting

Mark the quilting pattern on the quilt top. Take care not to crease the quilt. Layer the quilt top, batting, and backing. Then quilt the layers. The following patterns were used for BIRDS 'N' ROSES.

Stipple quilting. The center appliqué and the appliqué in the corner units have dense hand stipple quilting around them that does not need to be marked.

Echo quilting. In the center area, stippling gradually gives way to echo quilting, following the ribbon ring curves. Working from the ribbons toward the center, mark the echo lines ¾" apart. Fade out the lines at varying depths toward the center. A gradual change will be more pleasing than a definite line around the appliqué. As you quilt, add one or two stitching lines between the marked lines. The finished lines should be no more than ¼" apart, and preferably five or six rows to the inch.

Small flowers. Mark small flowers (pattern on page 100) randomly throughout the circular border. There are four small quilted flowers between each rosette.

Rose and feather quilting. Join the three pattern pieces (pages 101–103) to make a complete master pattern. Mark the rose and feather quilting pattern on the quilt top beyond the outer ribbon and loop ring.

Straight-line quilting. Mark radiating lines from the inner ribbon ring to the outer edge of the corner areas. At their outer reaches, the lines should be ¾" apart. The lines will be much closer together at the inner ribbon ring. Fade the lines out around the corner appliqué and replace them with stipple quilting.

Border quilting. Change the direction of the quilting in the border. Mark lines along the length of the border: mark two lines ¼" apart and leave ¾" between each pair of close lines.

Trapunto. When the quilting is complete, stuff some areas of the quilting (see photo right center). The random small flowers in the circular border should be firmly stuffed. Stuff the rose and feathers. Take great care not to overstuff or it will distort the shape of the quilt.

Finishing the Quilt

When the quilting is finished, take out the basting stitches and trim the edges of the quilt to ¼". Trim the batting and lining to between ⅜" and ½". Use the 360" blue strip and your preferred technique to bind the raw edges of the quilt. Add a label with your name, quilt name, and the date it was made on the back of the quilt.

Washing quilts is much a matter of personal preference. However, a quilt that has taken so long to make is unlikely to be clean. A gentle wash will freshen the fabrics and add an antique shrunken look to the quilting stitches.

Quilt label

Alternate Appliqué Patterns

Center flowers. The flower pattern on page 104 can be used in the center of the quilt in place of the two asymmetrical auricula rosettes The flowers of this pattern are not symmetrical, but the leaves are.

Center area. If you prefer, you can replace the whole center area with the pattern on pages 105–112. All rose stems and rose leaves will be identical, whereas they show some degree of variance in the original pattern. The radius of this center appliqué is 33", the same as the medallion on Birds 'n' Roses.

The center comprises four roses, with lilies and large leaves. The rest of the appliqué pieces are the same as those used in Birds 'n' Roses, with the exception of a few small leaves. Auriculas have been used but could be substituted by small blue bell-like flowers, which would create a quilt more like the original Garden Quilts.

Swag border. This swag fits around a circle, which is marked on the pattern (pages 113–115). The circle has a radius of 27". This swag can be substituted for the ribbon and loop rings and circular auricula border. It can also be used with other alternative patterns to make a traditional Garden Quilt.

Corner area. The corner unit on this page is similar to the example of a typical Garden Quilt on page 16. Allow 6" or 7" of plain fabric beyond the corners as a final plain border. Patterns are given on pages 116–125.

Birds 'n' Roses
Patterns

Margaret Docherty

Original Center Assembly
Alternate patterns begin on page 105.

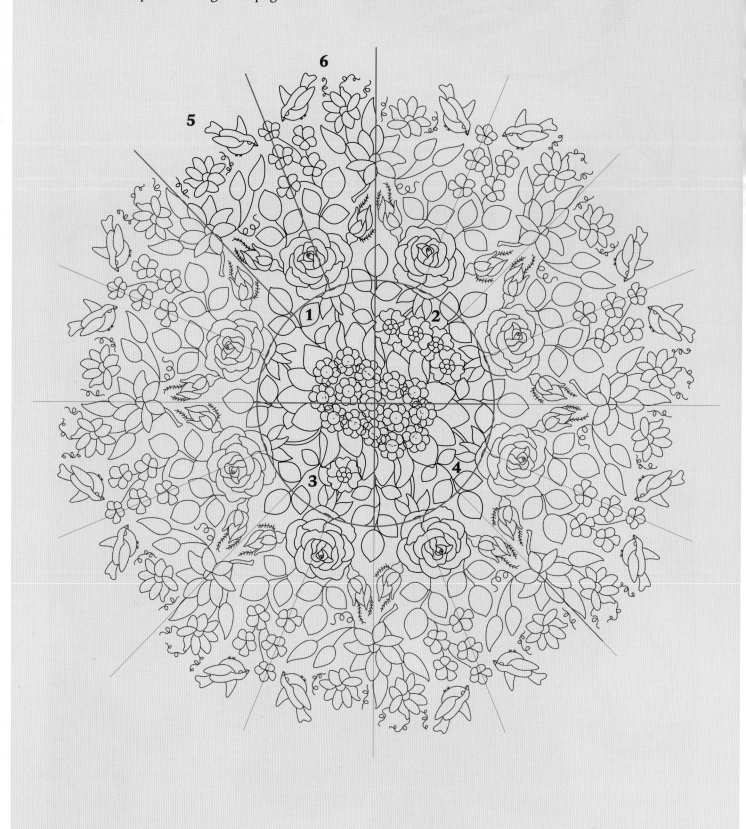

Margaret Docherty

Original Center – section 1 of 6

Original Center – section 2 of 6

Margaret Docherty

Original Center – section 3 of 6

Margaret Docherty

Original Center – section 4 of 6

Original Center – section 5 of 6

Margaret Docherty

Original Center – section 6 of 6

Margaret Docherty

Original Circular Border Assembly

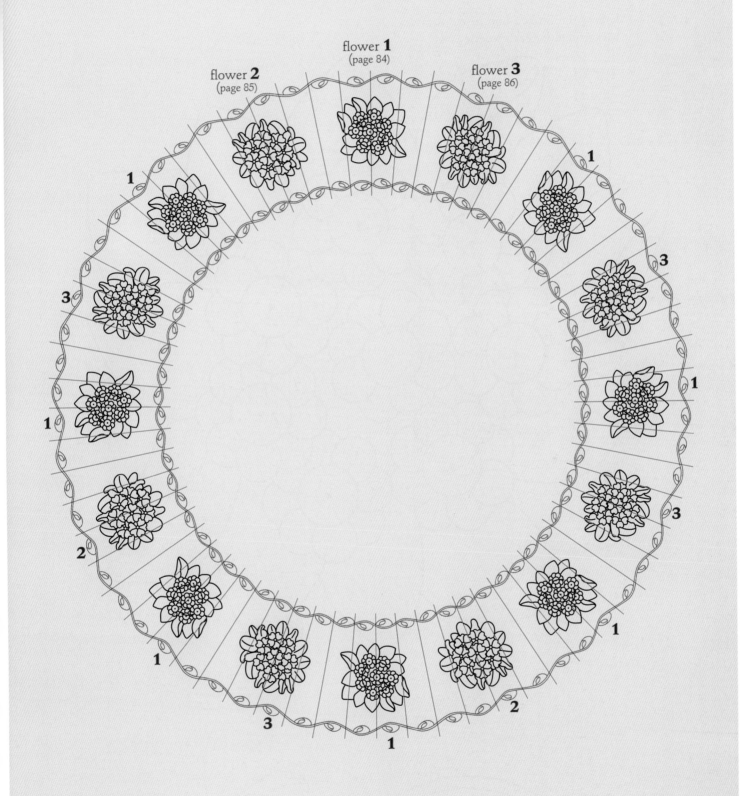

flower **2**
(page 85)

flower **1**
(page 84)

flower **3**
(page 86)

Original Circular Border – auriculas
flower **1**

Follow the broken line to cut a green
background for each rosette.

Original Circular Border – polyanthus with 6 petals
flower **2**

Original Circular Border – polyanthus with 5 petals
flower **3**

Original Circular Border – spacing between patterns

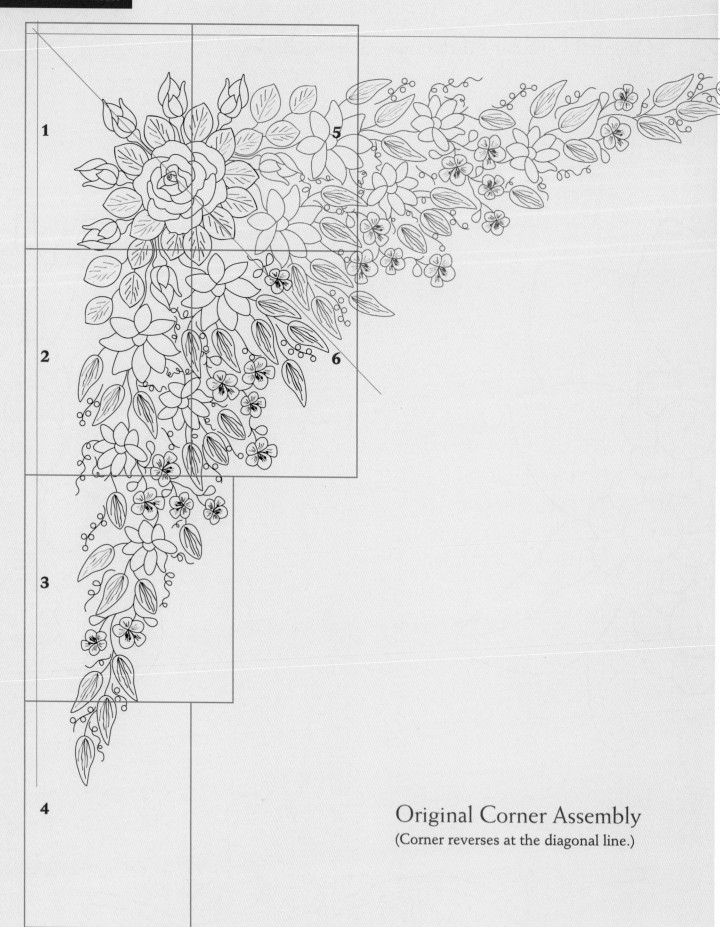

1

5

2

6

3

4

Original Corner Assembly
(Corner reverses at the diagonal line.)

Margaret Docherty

Original Corner – section 1 of 6

Margaret Docherty

Original Corner – section 2 of 6

Original Corner – section 3 of 6

Margaret Docherty

Original Corner – section 4 of 6

Margaret Docherty

Original Corner – section 5 of 6

Original Corner – section 6 of 6

Margaret Docherty

Outer Border Assembly

corner   geranium section   center

Outer Border – center section

center line

seam

Outer Border –
center extended showing bird placement

center line

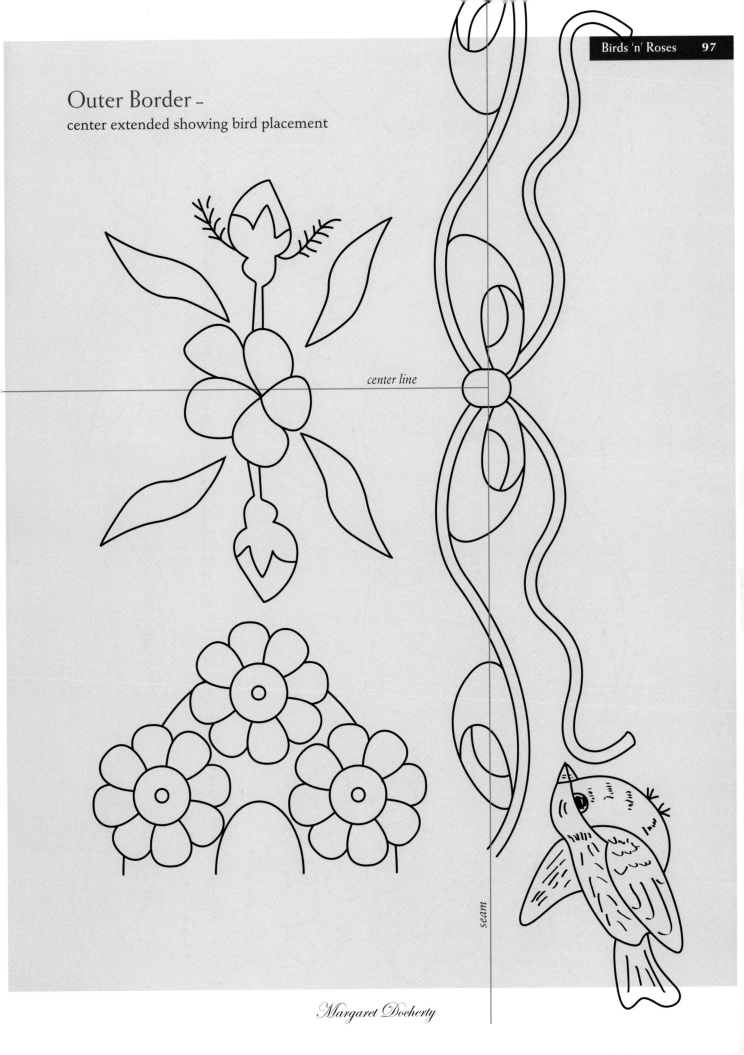

Margaret Docherty

Outer Border – geranium section

seam

Margaret Docherty

Outer Border – corner section

seam

corner line

Quilting for Circular Border

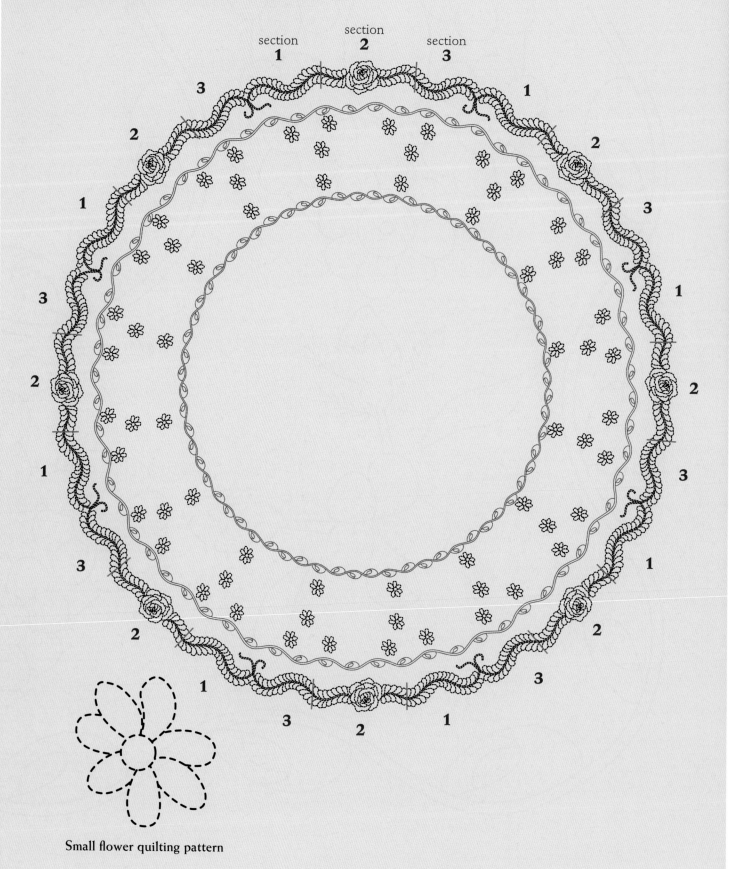

Small flower quilting pattern

Margaret Docherty

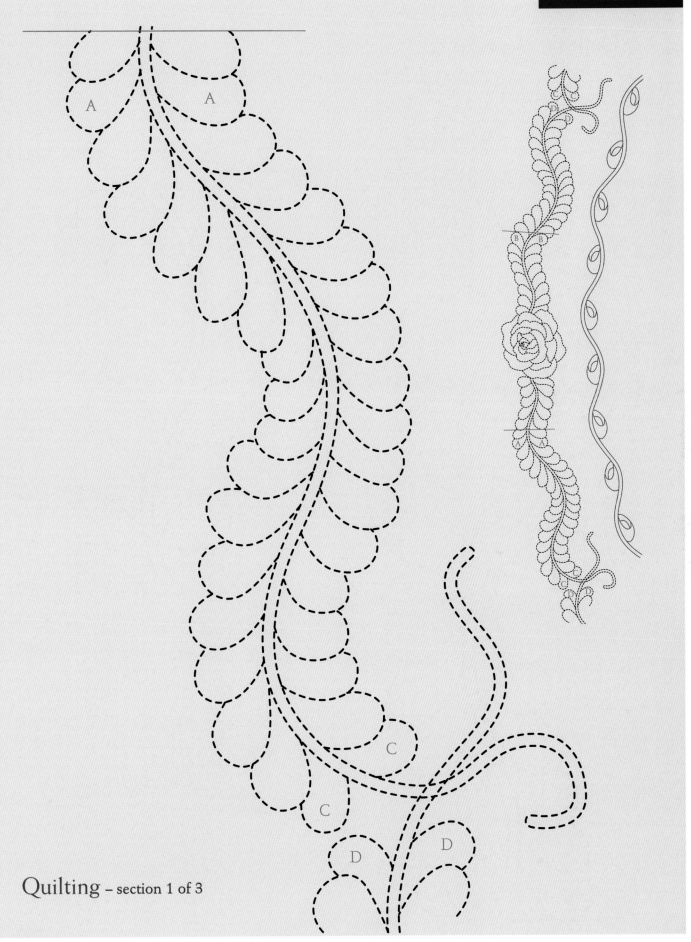

Quilting – section 1 of 3

Quilting – section 2 of 3

Quilting – section 3 of 3

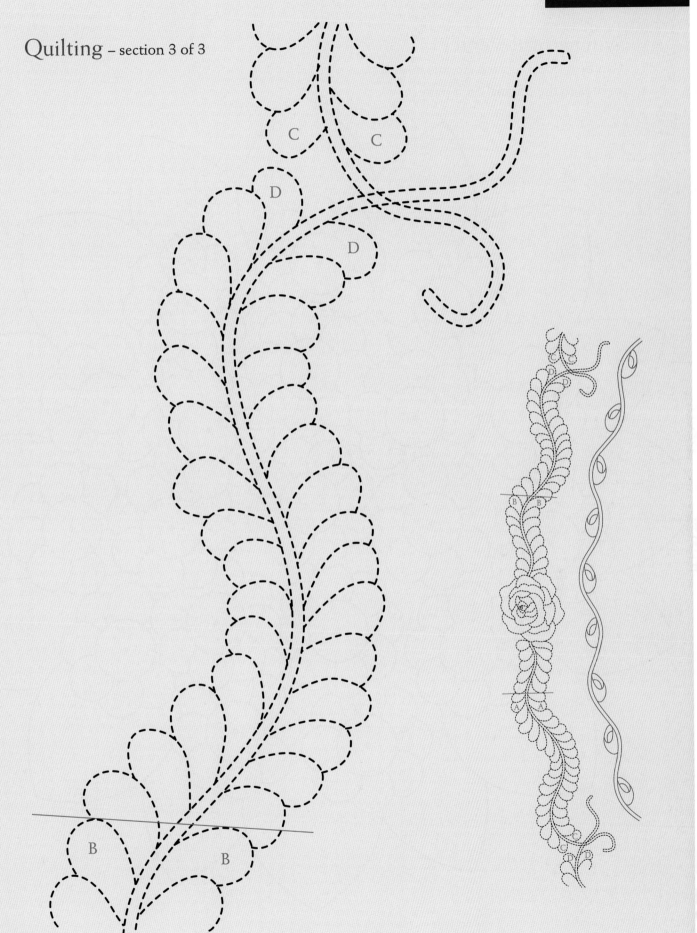

Margaret Docherty

Symmetrical Center –

Can be used to replace the two auricula
rosettes in the original quilt pattern.

Margaret Docherty

Alternate Appliqué Patterns

Alternate Center Assembly

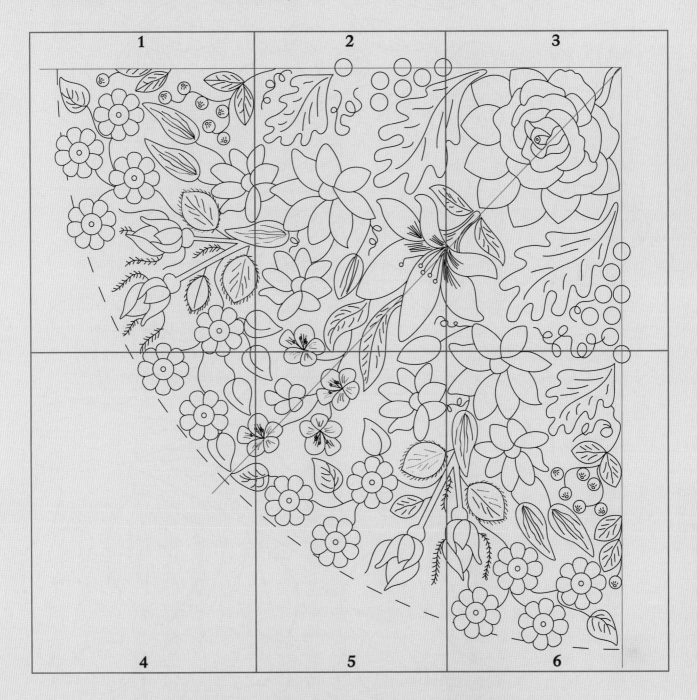

Alternate Center – section 1 of 6

Alternate Center – section 2 of 6

Margaret Docherty

Alternate Center – section 3 of 6

Alternate Center – section 4 of 6

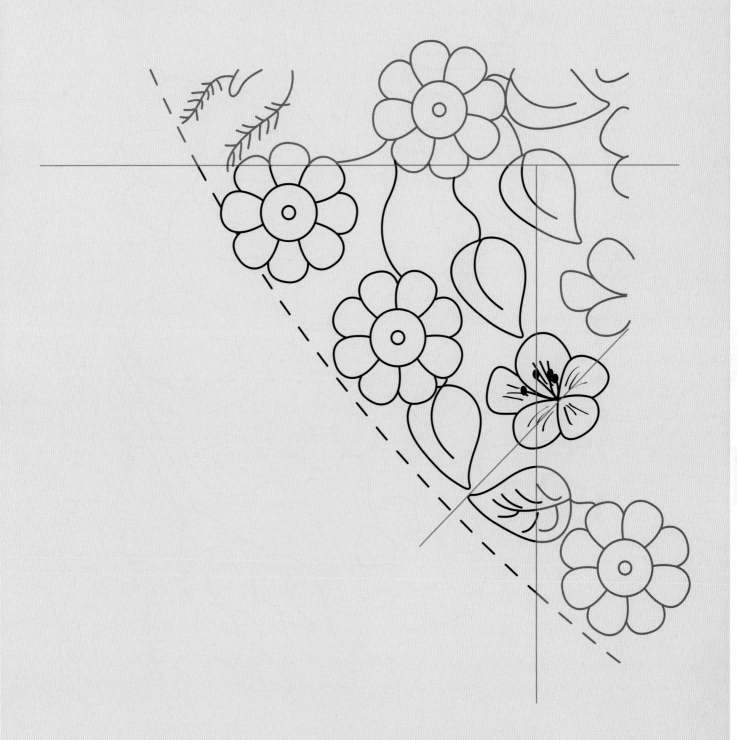

Margaret Docherty

Alternate Center – section 5 of 6

Margaret Docherty

Alternate Center – section 6 of 6

Alternate Center Assembly

Margaret Docherty

Alternate Swag Border Assembly

Margaret Docherty

Alternate Swag Border – swag

section of circle
radius 27"

Margaret Docherty

Alternate Swag Border – rose and ribbon

Margaret Docherty

Alternate Corner Assembly –

Corner pattern reverses at the diagonal line.

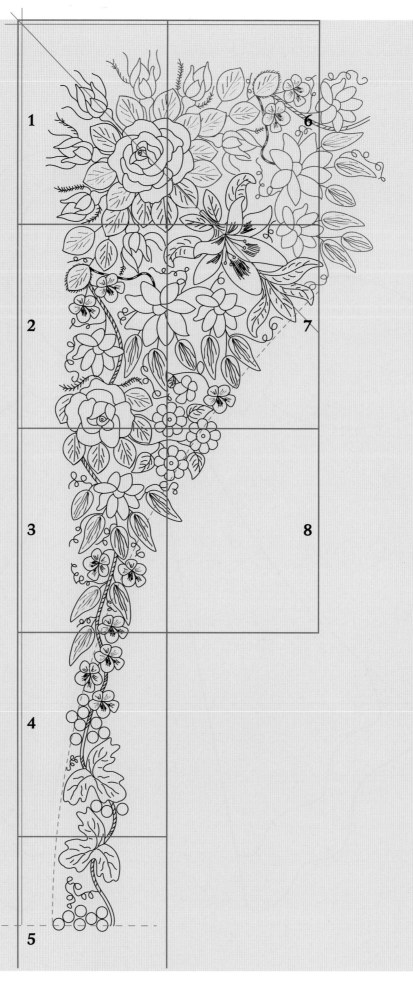

1

6

2

7

3

8

4

5

Margaret Docherty

Alternate Corner – section 1 of 8

Margaret Docherty

Alternate Corner – section 2 of 8

Alternate Corner – section 3 of 8

Margaret Docherty

Alternate Corner – section 4 of 8

Alternate Corner – section 5 of 8

Alternate Corner – section 6 of 8

Margaret Docherty

Alternate Corner – section 7 of 8

Margaret Docherty

Alternate Corner – section 8 of 8

Margaret Docherty

Alternate Corner Assembly

Margaret Docherty

Bibliography

Austin, Mary Leman, editor. *The Twentieth Century's Best American Quilts.* Golden, Colorado: Primedia, 1999.

Brackman, Barbara. *Clues in the Calico.* New York: EPM Communications, 1989.

— *Encyclopedia of Appliqué.* Howell Press, 1993.

Buckley, Karen Kay. *Appliqué Basics: Flower Wreaths.* Paducah, Kentucky: American Quilter's Society, 1999.

Docherty, Margaret. *Masterpiece Appliqué: Little Brown Bird Patterns.* Paducah, Kentucky: American Quilter's Society, 2000.

Finley, Ruth. *Old Patchwork Quilts and the Women Who Made Them.* Philadelphia: J. B. Lippincott Co.,1929.

Hall, Carrie, and Rose Kretsinger. *The Romance of the Patchwork Quilt in America.* New York: Bonanza Books, 1935.

Kirocofe, Roderick, and Mary Elizabeth Johnson. *The American Quilt, A History of Cloth and Comfort 1750—1950.* New York: Clarkson N. Potter, 2004.

Webster, Marie D. *Quilts: Their Story and How to Make Them.* Santa Barbara: Practical Patchwork, 1990.